LIVE AND LEARN AND PASS IT ON

◆

Volume II

People ages 5 to 95 share what they've discovered
about life, love, and other good stuff

Written and compiled by H. JACKSON BROWN, JR.

RUTLEDGE HILL PRESS
Nashville, Tennessee

Published in Nashville, Tennessee, by Rutledge Hill Press, Inc., 211 Seventh Avenue North, Nashville, Tennessee 37219. Distributed in Canada by H. B. Fenn & Company, Ltd., 1090 Lorimar Drive, Mississauga, Ontario L5S 1R7. Distributed in Australia by Millennium Books, 13/3 Maddox Street, Alexandria NSW 2015. Distributed in New Zealand by Tandem Press, 2 Rugby Road, Birkenhead, Auckland 10. Distributed in the United Kingdom by Verulam Publishing, Ltd., 152a Park Street Lane, Park Street, St. Albans, Hertfordshire AL2 2AU.

Typography by D&T/Bailey Typesetting, Inc., Nashville, Tennessee.

Library of Congress Cataloging-in-Publication Data

Live and learn and pass it on : people ages 5 to 95 share what they've learned about life, love, and other good stuff / written and compiled by H. Jackson Brown, Jr.

p. cm.

ISBN 1-55853-394-X (v. 2)

1. Life cycle, Human—Miscellanea. 2. Developmental psychology—Miscellanea. 3. Maturation (Psychology)—Miscellanea. I. Brown, H. Jackson, 1940– .

HQ799.95.L55   1991   158'.1   91-32132

Printed in the United States of America
1 2 3 4 5 6 7 8 9 — 99 98 97 96

INTRODUCTION

WHAT HAS life taught you? Would you share it with me?
That is the simple premise behind this book and its
predecessor.

In 1992 I compiled and edited the first volume of *Live and
Learn and Pass It On,* and on a whim I asked readers to send me
whatever wise sayings, humorous observations, and practical
advice they would like to share. Thousands of readers
accepted my invitation. This book is a collection of my
favorite responses, along with some of my own discoveries.

Here's a small sampling:

- on finance: *"I've learned that loaning money to friends and
  relatives causes them to get amnesia."*

- on self-esteem: *"I've learned that if you are in a relationship with
  someone who doesn't believe in you, you should get out before you
  stop believing in yourself."*

- on basic car maintenance: *"I've learned that when the oil light is on in your car, you really should put some oil in it!"*
- on skin care: *"I've learned that putting toothpaste on your zits will make them go away."*
- plus a few words on managing stress from an eleven-year-old: *"I've learned that when you are really stressed out, the cure is to put two miniature marshmallows up your nose and try to 'snort' them out."*

This little book represents what we human beings have been doing with a certain amount of success for the past million or so years, namely, living, learning, and passing it on.

Some of these lessons were not easily learned. Many were the culmination of years of experience. Still others came as spontaneous revelations. There is enough subtle wisdom on the following pages to interest a Zen master and enough comic material for a *Seinfeld* sitcom.

George Bernard Shaw once wrote, "Giving advice is like kissing; it doesn't cost anything and it is a pleasant thing to do." True enough. But *receiving* practical and witty advice can be highly pleasurable too, as I hope reading this little book will prove.

H.J.B.
Tall Pine Lodge
Fernvale, Tennessee

ACKNOWLEDGMENTS

MY GRATEFUL THANKS to all who contributed to this collection of discoveries and insights: Rosemary Brown, Adam Brown, Anna Abraham, Angela Adair, Marilyn J. Adams, DeAnn Adelman, Sherri Allen, Steven Anderson, Joanne Anderson, June Anderson, Jeff Armes, Anna Marie Rose Atienza, Janice Anita Austin, Colleen Bailey, Peggy Baillie, Sean Baltz, John Bancheri, Dean Stanton Barnard Jr., Karin M. Basso, Laura Williams Bell, Amy Benedetto, Margaret Berardinelli, Nicholas Berlanga, Laura Bernell, Stacey Berry, David Betten, Jewell K. Bevan, Patricia Birmingham, Katie Blaschko, Frederika Blasko, Carol Bolno, Lois Boyd, Sandy Bradbury, Betty Brady, Kristy Breedlove, Diana Britt, Beth Brochu, Allison Brown, Betty Brown, Nancy Brown, Maryann Brummel, Elizabeth Brunelle, Leslie Brydon, Karen Buchan, Yolanda Bucio, Alice Buret, Chip Burns, Christopher Bursian, Marie Burt, Katy Butler, Susan L. Butler, Lois Byrd, Laura Beth Byrne, Peggy Byrnes, SuAnne Cacamese, George E. Calfo, Jennifer Capone, Donna Canfield, Tree Carel, Bea Carmody, Kate Carroll, Melissa Carroll, Joseph Carubia, Douglas Casa, Mick Cassidy, Vincent Cautero, Jason Allen Cerezo, Sharon Circ, Will Chappell, Patricia Chu, Laurie Kristin Clark, Rebecca Cohen, Kasey Cole, Noni Coleman, Marilynn Collins, Jean Coneff, Ransom Converse, Karl L. G. Crose, Kelly L. Crawford, Erin Cox, Susanne Cox, Elektra Athena Dalrymple, Debbie Davidson, Kellie Dawson, Peggy Lee Dean, Jerry Deatherage, Stacia Deedrick, Michelle C. Defatta, Kristin June DeGiso, Virginia DeMars, Lawrence Dikeman, David W. Donovan, Deborah Dougherty, Deborah L. Dougal, Gwyndolin DuBose, Patricia Dugert, Cynthia Eichengreen, Vivian Elbert, Mary A. Elliott, Eleanor Emerson, Lindsey Emswiler, Lucille Everingham, Catie Fain, Jane B. Fawcett, Donny Ferritto, Rebecca Fillmore, Dawn Finley, Mary E. Finnerty, Vi Fishbaugh, Lisa Fischer, Ila Foley, Dana Ford, Robert Fox, Florence Freedman, Carolyn Jane Freeman, Edna B. Frisbie, Robert P. Fullmer, Karen Funkhouser, Jane Ellen Gaines, Jeannie George, Lisa Giaramita, Suanna Gibson, Mrs. Clayton Gillette, Selina Gilliam, Arlene Glass, Kristina Glicksman, Adam Goertzen, Judith Goodchild, Barbara Goodman, Cathy Gorsuch, Diane Grabhorn, Mary Grabowski, Mary Row Gravely, MaryBeth Greaney, Cynthia Green, Mary Jo Grill, Jo Marie Grinkiewicz, Eileen Gromada, Ricky Groom, Karl Grose, Teresa Gunter, Ruth Hahner, Robert Haley, Shannon Halley, Joyce Hanes, Carla Hanks, Ndala G. Harper, Walt Harper, Albert Harris, Holly Haukaas, Mary Haynes, Margaret Hedlund, Lynn Hellman, Robert Hendrick, H. A. Henrich, Chip Herin, Daisy Hersey-Orr, Sage Holben, Julie Horkheimer, Bernilda Hoth, Frederich Hovey Jr., Nicole Howard, Diana Hughes, Martin Hughes, Kellie Huse, Janet Jackson, Tammy Jackson,

Susan Jeffery, Francis Johnson, Gala Jones, Holly Jones, Jennifer Jones, Shirley Jordan, Anitura Joseph, Regina Joy, Stacy Judd, Robert Jutte-Kraus, Jenne Keller, Ruth S. Kelley, Paige Kepner, Dawn King, Karie Kinskey, Paul Koehler, Meredith Lynn Kohut, Erin Kossoris, Kenneth Kovac, Alisa Krintz, Tracy L. Kundinger, Edna B. Laine, Jessie Lang, Robert LaPlante, Amy Lazarus, Angela Lechter, Shanna Lewis, Lucy Limberis, Judity A. Lindberg, Brandon Long, Elizabeth Lopato, Linda Lopes, Estela Lugo, Patricia Lukoschek, Greg Lumpkin, Nicole Lusby, Wendy Lutz, Tiana Lyles, Heather Lytwyn, Ryan MacMichael, Colleen Magistad, Jason Malay, Susan Masaitis, Diane K. Mason, M. C. Martindale, Mari-Job Maulit, Kathy Maurer, Susan May, Greg Mayer, Susan Mayer, Sarah McBride, Shirley McCallum, Betty McClure, Kellian McDermott, Teresa McDowell, Gyneth McGarvey, Pam McGee, Cynthia N. McGivern, Pat McGovern, Kellie McInnis, Maureen McKenzie, Alline K. McNeil, Joan McQuerry, Susan Mechler, Maureen Melia, Imy Menser, Sylvia Moffett, Frances Miller-Papenfuss, Lara L. Milne, Sushine D. Montgomery, Lynn Moore, Michelle Morgan, Kristi Morse, John Mortes, Julia Mulane, Hillary Munn, Sarah Ann Nelson, Michael Kelly Newsome, Anh Nguyen, Kim Nicely, Darcy Nichols, Irene Noraas, Meg Northcut, Jack Nussbaum, Kimberly Olson, Joan Onzo, Raymond J. Ormand, Irene Packard, Esther B. Palmer, Lucille Parker, Madeline Parker, Lena Parmiter, Florence Paulie-Healy, Amy Peacher, William Peredina, Jo Carole Peters, Adam Phillips, Wendy Pitlik, Nikki Plant, John Preston, Dan Prezembel, Lisa Quatrini, Carrie, Rahm, Elizabeth Rakowski, Karen Reinerston, Janelle Rice, Stephanie Robson, Pat Rodgers, Peter Rogers, Jolynn Ruud, Janice H. Ryan, Rene Rylander, Frances Sagona, Theresa Salak-Fawcett, Christine Sales, Fred Salter, Judy Sawyer, Vassa Scales, Eva Schmitz, Darch Schouw, Burton Schwartz, Rick Schwab, Drew Searing, Kelly Seelye, Elise Selinger, Eleanor Wright Shabica, Nell Shaffer, Carol Shahla, Eric S. Sherman, Ruby E. Shine, Shannon M. Skroback, Jean Slight, Cynthia Snell, Laurie Lynn Snyder, Paula Snyder, Andrew Sopko, Diane Spangler, Jane Spens, Cindy Standlee, Liz Starke, Amy Diane Steiner, Audrey L. Steiner, Jacquelyn Stone, Bob Sullivan, Valerie Sussek, Katy Swann, Jennifer Swanson, Tara Swanson, Erika Sweek, Keri Sweet, Kelly Tankersley, Beth Theriot, Stephanie Tignor, Rick Tobe, Beverly Tomsic, Christine E. Torres, Frances S. Townes, Tami Tronick, Naohiko Tsukada, Kendra Turnbow, Terry Tyson, Nancy Vanhamel, Ricky Villabona, Pat Wade, Mark Walker, Kristine Wallace, Janet M. Wasilewski, J. Avis Waterbury, Erika L. Watt, Shirley Watts, Carol Webster, Rachel Wehner, Eric Welch, Tami Westhoff, Jerry White, Carol Lynn Whiteley, Elissa Wickman, Rebecca Wiley, Paula Williams, Eleanor Wilson, Erica Wilson, Jennifer Winters, Darryl Wisher, Abby Wood, Kelly Workman, Heather Wrigley, Jennifer C. Wroe, and Lynn Younglove.

Other Books by H. Jackson Brown, Jr.

A Father's Book of Wisdom
P.S. I Love You
Life's Little Instruction Book
Live and Learn and Pass It On
Life's Little Instruction Book, Volume II
Life's Little Treasure Book on Joy
Life's Little Treasure Book on Marriage and the Family
Life's Little Treasure Book on Wisdom
Life's Little Treasure Book on Success
Life's Little Treasure Book on Parenting
Life's Little Treasure Book on Love
When You Lick a Slug, Your Tongue Goes Numb
The Little Book of Christmas Joys
(with Rosemary Brown and Kathy Peel)
Life's Little Instruction Book, Volume III

I've learned that home is the place where we grumble the most and are loved the best.
—Age 89

I've learned that I shouldn't get out of the shower to answer the phone. It will stop ringing the minute I get to it.
—Age 53

I've learned that first graders are the only ones who think it's neat when their teeth fall out.
—Age 25

I've learned that drinking a Diet Coke doesn't make up for the candy bar I enjoyed earlier.

—Age 19

I've learned that the closest I get to living in the fast lane is when I'm going through the express lane in the supermarket.

—Age 69

I've learned that it makes me happy to see the answering machine light flashing when I get home.

—Age 18

I've learned that you should never put off saying, "I love you," in any relationship as long as you sincerely mean it. Otherwise, you may spend the rest of your life regretting it.

—Age 19

I've learned that getting up early is a problem for me and my mom.

—Age 7

I've learned that when the traffic signal light says "walk," I'd better run.

—Age 57

I've learned that I should never have taught my four-year-old sister how to load and shoot my BB gun.
—Age 12

I've learned that I should never tell my husband bad news on an empty stomach.
—Age 60

I've learned that when my house is the messiest my mother-in-law will drop by.
—Age 29

I've learned that loaning money to friends
and relatives causes them to get amnesia.

—Age 32

I've learned that if you are in a relationship
with someone who doesn't believe in you,
you should get out before you stop
believing in yourself. *—Age 22*

I've learned that women will never
understand the Three Stooges. *—Age 15*

I've learned that just when I think I know everything, my son will ask me something I don't know or can't possibly explain. *—Age 28*

I've learned that when the oil light is on in your car, you really should put some oil in it!

—Age 23

I've learned that saying "hi" to somebody today can result in a new friend tomorrow.

—Age 18

I've learned that it's best to ask for what you need from your loved ones and not assume that *somehow* they'll just know.

—*Age 34*

I've learned that old age is not a defeat but a victory, not a punishment but a privilege.

—*Age 79*

I've learned that being an elementary teacher is the most noble profession of all.

—*Age 19*

I've learned that of all the bad four-letter words, DIET is the worst.

—*Age 54*

I've learned that the way to grow old gracefully is to keep active.

—*Age 82*

I've learned that no matter how old or how experienced you are, you can always learn something from a child.

—*Age 20*

I've learned that an act of love, no matter how great or small, is always appreciated.

—Age 22

I've learned that girls who won't hold frogs, snakes, and mice because it's not a girlish thing to do are missing something good.

—Age 17

I've learned that when planning a project, the shortest pencil is worth more than the longest memory.

—Age 38

I've learned that if these are supposed to be the best years of my life, I'm in for one bumpy ride.

—Age 16

I've learned that my husband's encouragement can make me do things I thought I couldn't.   —*Age 32*

I've learned that you should never buy white carpet if you have a black dog. —*Age 30*

I've learned that country music can always make me feel better when I'm melancholy because the people in the songs are always in a worse situation than I am.   —*Age 14*

I've learned that there are two words that will always draw a crowd: *free food.*   —*Age 82*

I've learned that you should always put on a new bathing suit and get it wet before wearing it in public.   —*Age 21*

I've learned that the importance of fame, fortune, and all other things pales in comparison to the importance of positive personal relationships.   —*Age 50*

I've learned that my best friend and I can do anything or nothing and have the best time.

—Age 18

I've learned that no situation is so bad that losing your temper won't make it worse.

—Age 71

I've learned that no matter how beautiful your makeup is, it can't hide the expression of a sad heart.

—Age 21

I've learned that most people don't look for the truths of life; they only search for someone to agree with them.

—Age 27

I've learned that having five brothers and one sister is really a great blessing, even though it has taken me sixteen years to figure out it was a blessing.　　　—*Age 16*

I've learned that everybody wants to be special to someone.　　　—*Age 22*

I've learned that if you have several tasks, do the hardest one first. Then the rest are a snap.　　　—*Age 86*

I've learned that if you leave clothes in the ironing pile long enough, you'll outgrow them and you can sell them in a yard sale.

—Age 57

I've learned that you can't believe everything you hear, even if you hear it twice.

—Age 18

I've learned that you'll never see a U-Haul trailer behind a hearse.

—Age 59

I've learned that although I can skip class without getting in trouble, there's still the consequence at exam time. —*Age 19*

I've learned that people can surprise you. Sometimes the people you expect to kick you when you're down will be the ones to help you get back up. —*Age 32*

I've learned that a woman can stand anything but being forgotten or not being needed. —*Age 89*

I've learned that warmth, kindness, and friendship are the most yearned for commodities in the world. The person who can provide them will never be lonely.

—*Age 79*

I've learned that picking out a lunch box for an eight-year-old is a major decision.

—*Age 30*

I've learned that it is never too late to start reading the Bible.

—*Age 34*

I've learned that the greatest test of
friendship is to take a vacation together
and still like each other when you return.

—Age 59

I've learned that the prayer I say most often
is, "Lord, please keep your arm around my
shoulder and your hand over my mouth."

—Age 34

I've learned that a minute of extra thinking
beforehand can save hours of worry later.

—Age 22

I've learned that when I'm acting really stupid and I think that no one's watching, the guy I want to impress is watching.

—Age 13

I've learned that all the advice and wisdom in the world cannot help you unless you apply it daily in your life. *—Age 23*

I've learned that if you throw ten socks in the laundry, only nine will come out. *—Age 27*

I've learned that a smile, a "How are you?"
and a warm, close, caring hug always give
love, faith, and hope.   —*Age 54*

I've learned that nothing feels as good as
my fiancé's arms around me when we've
been separated too long.   —*Age 19*

I've learned that you are never too old to
try something new.   —*Age 82*

I've learned that no matter how closely I follow her recipe, my cooking never tastes as good as my mom's.

—Age 24

I've learned that when you have problems operating your VCR, call in your five-year-old grandson.

—Age 73

I've learned that no matter how much a friend promises not to tell anyone else, she always does.

—Age 16

I've learned that I am the only one in my house who cleans the hair out of the drain in the shower.   *—Age 23*

I've learned that when I surprise an old friend with a phone call, it will seem like just yesterday that we last spoke.   *—Age 38*

I've learned that people place too much importance on progress and not enough on maintenance.   *—Age 32*

I've learned that the longer you have been in the car with your children, the harder it is to laugh at the jokes they tell.   —*Age 33*

I've learned that life is like a ten-speed bicycle. Most of us have gears we never use.   —*Age 59*

I've learned that you shouldn't leave your fork on your plate when you reheat your food in the microwave.   —*Age 13*

I've learned that it doesn't make any difference whether or not you name your cat. He never comes when called anyway.

—*Age 31*

I would rather have a best friend than a boyfriend, except maybe on a Friday night.

—Age 20

I've learned that you can't scramble eggs in the toaster oven.

—Age 14

I've learned that no matter how long it is between visits, when I see my sisters it's like it has been only a week, not years.

—Age 45

I've learned that you are not an adult until you accept responsibility for your own actions and quit blaming everything on the way your parents reared you. *—Age 37*

I've learned that it is no fun to watch television unless you have the remote control. *—Age 23*

I've learned that good or bad, most things don't last very long. *—Age 32*

I've learned that life is both simple and complicated at the same time. The trick is finding the simple truths that are contained in the complicated confusion. *—Age 24*

I've learned that an adult is someone who stopped growing, except in the middle.

—Age 72

I've learned that good habits are just as hard to break as bad habits. *—Age 62*

I've learned that no one ever drinks the last tablespoon of anything in a container they would have to wash or refill.   —*Age 49*

I've learned that the easiest way to find happiness is to quit complaining.   —*Age 19*

I've learned that grandmothers are still girls at heart. They like pats, hugs, and kisses.   —*Age 85*

I've learned that if you finish the toilet paper roll without replacing it, you will be the first person who needs it next. *—Age 18*

I've learned that having football games in the house isn't a good idea. *—Age 9*

I've learned that whatever color you like the least, your mother-in-law will love the most. *—Age 33*

I've learned that you can sit and worry until you are physically ill, but worrying doesn't change things—action does.   *—Age 46*

I've learned that absent-minded people get lots of exercise looking for things they can't find.   *—Age 66*

I've learned that doctors deserve and appreciate thank-you notes.   *—Age 21*

I've learned that you should keep an open mind, but don't be so open-minded that your brains fall out.

—Age 54

I've learned that perspective is everything. To a worm, digging in the hard ground is more relaxing than going fishing. —*Age 65*

I've learned that good quality underwear is worth the extra cost. —*Age 25*

I've learned that there is no joy like the joy of seeing a child learn to read. —*Age 18*

I've learned that taking a break in the middle of a job is not half as relaxing as taking a break after the job is finished.

—Age 16

I've learned that some people love talking about history, especially their own. *—Age 64*

I've learned that I am grateful for what I've learned, no matter what it cost me. *—Age 34*

I've learned that life with my husband's faults is hands down better than life without my husband.

—Age 49

I've learned that nothing makes your heart rejoice more than children, all ages and colors, playing happily together on a playground at recess.

—Age 19

I've learned that the best place to fill the sugar bowl is over the sink.

—Age 78

I've learned that I'm getting more and more like my mom, and I'm kind of happy about it.

—Age 19

I've learned that some people can spend years putting off a ten-minute job. *—Age 16*

I've learned that the best part of the day is when my daughters first get home from school and we talk about their day. *—Age 34*

I've learned that my mom is always right about my boyfriends. *—Age 22*

I've learned that you should hope and work, but never hope more than you work.

—*Age 59*

I've learned that if you're not willing to move mountains for your friends, they won't be willing to move them for you.

—*Age 18*

I've learned that you can gain two pounds by eating half a pound of fudge. —*Age 16*

I've learned that you're asking for trouble when you leave a three-year-old in the car with the keys in the ignition. *—Age 33*

I've learned that not everyone can be silly. Some people just don't know how. *—Age 35*

I've learned that a mother is only as happy as her child. *—Age 49*

I've learned that sometimes when I'm angry I have the right to be angry, but that doesn't give me the right to be cruel. —*Age 42*

I've learned that I can tell a lot about people by what items they notice in my home.   —*Age 45*

I've learned that you should assemble a baby crib in the room where you intend to use it. It won't fit through the door fully assembled.   —*Age 35*

I've learned that my mom was right about life when she commented, "No one ever said it would be easy."

—Age 30

I've learned that nothing in the world looks as precious as a sleeping child.

—Age 34

I've learned that true friendship continues to grow, even over the longest distance.

—Age 19

I've learned that you shouldn't eat in a restaurant where the cook is skinny. *—Age 55*

I've learned that nothing will help you stick to a diet more than people telling you how good you are looking. *—Age 23*

I've learned that putting toothpaste on your zits will make them go away. *—Age 18*

I've learned that if either of
your parents are angry,
don't—and I repeat don't—
ask for money.   *—Age 10*

I've learned that just because someone doesn't love you the way you want them to doesn't mean they don't love you with all they have.

—Age 32

I've learned that the best way to learn something is to teach it to someone else.

—Age 20

I've learned that one of the best things I can give a hurting friend is my presence, not my words.

—Age 38

I've learned that when my dog or my children are feeling very insecure, they follow me everywhere—including into the bathroom.

—Age 42

I've learned that sometimes a P.S. to a letter contains the most important message of all.

—Age 14

I've learned that the best and often the most neglected advice I receive is from my mother.

—Age 22

I've learned that there is a great feeling of satisfaction in checking off the final item on my "Things to do today" list.   —*Age 34*

I've learned that when you have an older brother who is much larger than you, he is always right.   —*Age 15*

I've learned that it is easy to meet interesting people in bookstores.   —*Age 54*

I've learned that if you keep your husband's coffee cup filled as you travel, you will never have to ask to stop at a rest area.

—Age 50

I've learned that ranch dressing tastes good on anything.

—Age 19

I've learned that two retired people cannot live in harmony with a single-control electric blanket.

—Age 68

I've learned that when you have spilled
something on yourself, the first person to
tell you is the last person you see at the end
of the day. *—Age 25*

I've learned that a kindness given to one
person is contagious and will be passed
along. *—Age 50*

I've learned that it's worth fighting for
causes, but not with people. *—Age 40*

I've learned that you shouldn't hold important conversations in bathrooms. You never know who is hiding in the next stall.

—Age 14

I've learned that a good friend is the one who tells you how you really look in your jeans.

—Age 25

I've learned that the less time I have to work with, the more things I get done.

—Age 19

I've learned that having a young friend
when you are old is a special joy.   —*Age 83*

I've learned that most of my regrets
concern things I didn't do, and so now
I'm more likely to say, "Why not?" instead
of "no."   —*Age 53*

I've learned that no matter how much I
care, sometimes some people just don't
care back.   —*Age 18*

I've learned that it is best to give advice in only two circumstances: when it is requested and when it is a life-threatening situation.

—Age 61

I've learned that no matter how old I am, I want my mother when I'm hurting.   *—Age 31*

I've learned that putting things in a safe place doesn't mean you can find them again when you look.

—Age 58

I've learned that if you die broke, the timing was right.
—*Age 64*

I've learned that when you buy a musical instrument, never attempt to economize. Buy the best you can afford from a reputable dealer. A cheap instrument will never express the music that is in your heart.
—*Age 39*

I've learned that stain-resistant carpet will stain.
—*Age 10*

I've learned that sending my mother flowers on my birthday with a card saying "Happy Birthday with Love" makes her happy.

—Age 40

I've learned that you don't know the value of a dollar until you've earned it yourself.

—Age 17

I've learned that marriage is not always easy. You have to work on it more than anything else in life in order to make it successful.

—Age 26

I've learned that it's hard to kiss when you are smiling.

—Age 59

I've learned that a happy journey almost always depends on choosing the right companion.

—Age 65

I've learned that when packing for a vacation, you should take half as many clothes as you think you will need and twice as much money. Your clothes and money should run out about the same time!

—Age 55

I've learned that you should never go up a ladder with just one nail. *—Age 63*

I've learned that I was part of the mess. Both children are gone, and there are still crumbs on the kitchen counter and floor.

—Age 44

I've learned that we spend too much time wishing for things we don't have, and missing the things we do. *—Age 15*

I've learned that when you're too busy for your friends, you're too busy. *—Age 48*

I've learned that you should never be a passenger on a one-seat bicycle. *—Age 17*

I've learned that maturity has more to do with what types of experiences you've had and what you've learned from them, and less to do with how many birthdays you've celebrated. *—Age 27*

I've learned that an afternoon in my garden is better than an afternoon with a therapist.

—Age 37

I've learned that a warm smile beams,
"Welcome to this moment."

—Age 50

I've learned that you should never tell a
child that his dreams are unlikely or
outlandish. Few things are more
humiliating, and what a tragedy it would
be if he believed it.

—Age 18

I've learned that after winning an
argument with my wife, the first thing I
should do is apologize.

—Age 52

I've learned that doing something as a volunteer makes you feel better than if you were paid to do it.

—Age 16

I've learned that everyone wants to live on top of the mountain, but all the happiness and growth occurs while you're climbing it.

—Age 57

I've learned that the love that accompanies the birth of a child exceeds your greatest expectation.

—Age 27

I've learned that you have to listen to your brain. It has lots of information. —*Age 7*

I've learned that when writing letters to family and friends, if I put a quote, verse, or poem on the outside of the envelope, it's like sending a warm hug through the mail.

—*Age 50*

I've learned that although nobody admits to liking to have their picture taken, everyone secretly does. —*Age 32*

I've learned that having a child late in life can be the best thing that ever happened to you.
—Age 48

I've learned that your family doesn't always want to be there for you. It may seem funny, but other people you're not even related to can take care of you and love you and teach you to trust people again. Families aren't biological.
—Age 25

I've learned that whining doesn't solve problems.
—Age 10

I've learned that no matter how hard I try, chocolate chip cookie dough never makes it to the oven.

—Age 24

I've learned not to slide down wooden stairs with my sled.

—Age 7

I've learned that nothing makes me feel prettier than when a guy holds the door for me.

—Age 15

I've learned that all the advice in the world doesn't help some situations. There are many things we have to figure out on our own.

—Age 24

I've learned that those who reach their goals too easily have aimed too low. *—Age 73*

I've learned that children need a lot more smiles and hugs than lectures and instructions.

—Age 48

I've learned that there is no honesty like the honesty of a young child.

—Age 23

I've learned that when your newly born grandchild holds your little finger in his little fist, you're hooked for life.   —*Age 74*

I've learned that you should stop asking people for what they cannot give you and be content with what they can give.   —*Age 35*

I've learned that you should never take out your teeth when flushing the commode.

—*Age 72*

I've learned that your grandparents are always happy to see you, but they are even happier to see you go home. *—Age 12*

I've learned that children follow examples, not advice. *—Age 62*

I've learned that nobody wants to know what you're doing until you're doing something that you don't want anyone to know. *—Age 28*

I've learned that a compliment is appreciated by everyone.

—Age 34

I've learned that it's a very bad idea to telephone someone when you are angry with him. You should always wait until the next day—always.

—Age 18

I've learned that a peacock today may be a feather duster tomorrow.

—Age 62

I've learned that a mother never quite leaves her children at home, even when she doesn't take them along.

—*Age 62*

I've learned that to accomplish much is to accomplish a little each day.

—*Age 56*

I've learned that you should find out what a button is connected to before pushing it.

—*Age 21*

I've learned that rainy Sundays are great for snuggling, reading, napping, and watching old movies—but not necessarily in that order.

—Age 44

I've learned that a smile is an inexpensive way to improve your looks.

—Age 17

I've learned that I can't choose how I feel, but I can choose what I do about it.

—Age 28

I've learned that if someone asks, "How are you doing?" it's not necessary to give them a full report.

—Age 65

I've learned that picking out a Halloween pumpkin is fun at any age.

—Age 26

I've learned that I never have insomnia when it is time to get up in the morning.

—Age 57

I've learned that you should never jump off a diving board when you are wearing a bikini.

—Age 11

I've learned that students who pay their own way through college never flunk out.

—Age 55

I've learned that no matter how good a friend someone is, they're going to hurt you every once in a while, and you must forgive them for that.

—Age 18

I've learned that I wish I could have told
my mom that I love her one more time
before she passed away. *—Age 49*

I've learned that it is just as wrong to be
rude to a child as to an adult. In fact, it
may be more unforgivable. *—Age 52*

I've learned that what you pass on to your
children will affect generations. *—Age 60*

I've learned that at age twenty I had no brains but a nice body and at thirty I had brains and too much body. *—Age 34*

I've learned that it's hard to lie when you are looking into your mother's eyes. *—Age 9*

I've learned that I drive faster when a good song comes on the radio. *—Age 22*

I've learned that you shouldn't judge people too quickly. Sometimes they have a good reason for the way they act. *—Age 20*

I've learned that little children are more work physically and teenagers are more work emotionally. *—Age 40*

I've learned that you can learn to tap dance at the age of sixty-four. *—Age 65*

I've learned that after being on a diet for two weeks, all I lose is fourteen days.

—Age 60

I've learned that I shouldn't play with mom's glue gun on the dining room table.

—Age 7

I've learned that a homemade banana cream pie will impress men more than a new dress and a fancy hairdo.   *—Age 44*

I've learned that every wedding involves at least one argument between a bride and her mother.

—Age 25

I've learned that girls burp as much as boys.

—*Age 11*

I've learned that I should try to keep my words soft and tender, because tomorrow I may have to eat them.

—*Age 83*

I've learned that when I get close to people who are full of anger, their anger spills over onto me. But when I get close to people who are full of love, their love spills over onto me.

—*Age 57*

I've learned that in this world, you don't need a multitude of friends. All you really need is one who will stand by you through thick and thin.

—Age 34

I've learned that the greatest physician in the world is optimism.

—Age 41

I've learned that when you harbor bitterness, happiness will dock elsewhere.

—Age 38

I've learned
that there
are good
neighbors
wherever
you live.
—Age 30

I've learned that getting in the kitchen and cooking a healthy meal with the radio on relaxes me at the end of a stressful day.

—Age 36

I've learned that in a college dorm sleeping is the only way to get some time to yourself.

—Age 20

I've learned that men don't know what to do when a woman cries.

—Age 30

I've learned that my hair always looks good on the day I have an appointment to have it cut.

—Age 25

I've learned that there is nothing better than my dog waiting for me on the front porch, wagging his tail when I get home.

—Age 18

I've learned that I shouldn't say, "I don't care for that last piece of pie" when I really want it.

—Age 62

I've learned that you should never change everything in your life at once. Keep something the same just for stability so that it's easier to remember who you are. —*Age 40*

I've learned that your "I can" is more important than your "IQ." —*Age 14*

I've learned that true happiness is when your newborn sleeps through the night.

—*Age 30*

I've learned that it is just as much fun at age sixty-five to ride a carousel as it is to ride one at age five.

—Age 67

I've learned that you shouldn't waste too much of today worrying about yesterday.

—Age 45

I've learned that no matter how much I complain about it, my husband's snoring is one of the safest sounds I know.

—Age 21

I've learned that Santa Claus has good years and bad years.

—Age 10

I've learned that you shouldn't marry a man simply because the rest of your family is in love with him.

—Age 31

I've learned that mileage wears out an automobile while walking three miles a day keeps the body in shape.

—Age 70

I've learned that life is tough, but I'm tougher.

—Age 39

I've learned that nothing beats the taste of a slab of your own homemade bread fresh from the oven, slathered with a spoonful of your own homemade jam.

—Age 67

I've learned that opportunities are never lost; someone will take the one you miss.

—Age 89

I've learned that if you
pray for your enemies,
you will stop hating them.

—Age 74

I've learned that no one is perfect until you fall in love with him. —*Age 18*

I've learned that when my desk is clean and organized, I can't find anything. —*Age 20*

I've learned that some people go for brains and some for beauty, but everyone appreciates a good sense of humor. —*Age 30*

I've learned that I learned more in my college dorm than I did in any classroom.

—Age 26

I've learned that men would rather be lost for hours than stop and ask for directions.

—Age 30

I've learned that there's nothing sweeter than sleeping with your babies and feeling their breath on your cheeks.

—Age 38

I've learned that what matters is not that you be the best, but that you try your best.

—Age 15

I've learned that I like to plant my neighbors' favorite flowers in my flower boxes so that they can see and enjoy them.

—Age 50

I've learned that even if you've never had a pimple on the end of your nose before, one will show up there a week before the prom.

—Age 17

I've learned that marrying an extrovert
when you are an introvert can be good
for you.

—Age 35

I've learned that the airport rental car
shuttle service you use is always the last to
arrive.

—Age 51

I've learned that people love to get letters
from friends and family, no matter what the
subject is or the length of the letters. *—Age 22*

I've learned that I appreciate my mother a lot more since I became a mother.   —*Age 31*

I've learned that both a young child and an old person can make me feel young.   —*Age 48*

I've learned that the patience and love you show your children will surface when they reach the age of thirty.   —*Age 63*

I've learned that everyone you meet
deserves that first smile.

—Age 23

I've learned that when my child gets upset, he calms down much sooner if I stay calm.

—Age 33

I've learned that the fire of a past love will always burn with a small flame.   *—Age 18*

I've learned that the kind of adults my children are now is directly related to the kind of children I continually told them they were.

—Age 50

I've learned that you can have the most interesting conversations while having your teeth cleaned.

—Age 18

I've learned that I always think of the right thing to say when it's too late.

—Age 30

I've learned that it gives me great pleasure to write "what's the best thing that happened to me today" in my daily journal.

—Age 72

I've learned that commercials for feminine products always come on when you are sitting in the living room with men.   *—Age 19*

I've learned that one of the best things you can do for your children is introduce them to books.   *—Age 30*

I've learned that the easiest way for me to grow as a person is to surround myself with people smarter than I am.   *—Age 50*

I've learned that when I walk into my room at the end of the day, I always feel better when my bed is made. *—Age 21*

I've learned that when your wife simply answers, "nothing" when you ask her what's wrong, you're in deep trouble. *—Age 37*

I've learned that love, not time, heals all wounds. *—Age 14*

I've learned that you view other people's children in a whole different light when you have one of your own.   —*Age 35*

I've learned that even if you move fifteen hundred miles away, your mother still tells you what to do and you still feel as if you have to do it.   —*Age 21*

I've learned that having good hair is better than having good legs.   —*Age 19*

I've learned that adding extra spices can't cover those cooking mistakes. *—Age 46*

I've learned that people always underestimate my ability, but one thing they should never underestimate is the drive behind my ability. *—Age 25*

I've learned that when your phone doesn't ring, you should ring someone else's. *—Age 35*

I've learned that to ignore the facts does *not* change the facts.
—*Age 56*

I've learned that I get a lump in my throat every time I think of the day when my daughter will marry.
—*Age 44*

I've learned that when you plan to get even with someone, you are only letting the person who has hurt you to hurt you longer.
—*Age 13*

I've learned that if you want to remember the date of your wedding anniversary forever, just forget it once.

—Age 59

I've learned that I wouldn't feel eighty-five years old if I didn't look in the mirror.

—Age 85

I've learned that when you want a garment to shrink, it won't, and when you don't, it will come out of the dryer and fit your cat!

—Age 40

I've learned that you
should never lend your
allowance to your brother.

—Age 11

I've learned that a handmade quilt gives comfort as well as warmth.

—Age 46

I've learned that my mom brags when she gets the TV remote control.

—Age 10

I've learned that it isn't always enough to be forgiven by others. Sometimes you have to learn to forgive yourself.

—Age 20

I've learned that whenever I go to grandma's house, I come home with at least a dollar in change.

—Age 9

I've learned that if you are still talking about what you did yesterday, you haven't done much today.

—Age 21

I've learned that I shouldn't confuse the green tube of Ben-Gay with the green tube of hemorrhoidal ointment.

—Age 50

I've learned that when your five-year-old lies down on the couch, she's sick.   *—Age 37*

I've learned that when my best girlfriend tells me she's angry with her boyfriend and it's okay if I go out with him, she doesn't mean it.   *—Age 61*

I've learned that the best way to eat oatmeal is to feed it to the dog while my parents aren't looking.   *—Age 14*

I've learned that when someone gives you something, never say, "You shouldn't have."

—Age 50

I've learned that I shouldn't go shopping when I'm depressed. I always buy too much.

—Age 30

I've learned that it's fun to brighten someone's day by surprising her with a plate of homemade chocolate chip cookies.

—Age 20

I've learned that the Lord didn't do it all in one day. What makes me think I can?

—*Age 46*

I've learned that successful parenting is convincing each child that he is your favorite.

—*Age 57*

I've learned to gather all the crumbs thrown my way. They soon form a lovely, thick slice of life and memories.

—*Age 92*

I've learned that your ACT test score doesn't predict the rest of your life. —*Age 18*

I've learned that you shouldn't judge a person unless you have talked to him one on one. —*Age 11*

I've learned never to humiliate another person. Always give him an honorable way to back down or out of something and still save face. —*Age 25*

I've learned that you don't really know
someone until you've been to a casino
together.
                                    —*Age 46*

I've learned that dinner rolls bake a lot
faster if the oven is turned on.
                                    —*Age 37*

I've learned that when I feel down, nothing
quite picks me up like an "I'm proud of
you" from my mom.
                                    —*Age 22*

I've learned that no matter how bad your heart is broken, the world does not stop for your grief.

—Age 21

I've learned that when someone says, "I love you," she's really asking, "Do you love me?"

—Age 23

I've learned that if for nothing else, boyfriends are good for squishing those big brown spiders that appear in the bathtub.

—Age 24

I've learned that under everyone's hard shell is someone who wants to be appreciated and loved.

—Age 18

I've learned that you should never hire a plumber who bites his fingernails or an electrician who has singed eyebrows.

—Age 72

I've learned that you're never too old to learn something from *Sesame Street.*   *—Age 21*

I've learned that little boys cry more than little girls when getting shots. —*Age 75*

I've learned that children, no matter what their age, are always hungry when they go to grandma's house. —*Age 25*

I've learned that the best compliment my children gave me was when they said they would like to have a marriage like my husband's and mine. —*Age 72*

I've learned that no matter what their ages or how far away they may be, you never stop wanting to keep a protective arm around your children.

—Age 67

I've learned that when I want advice, I call my best friend. When I want sympathy, I call my boyfriend.

—*Age 48*

I've learned that you shouldn't let a day pass without making at least one person feel good.

—*Age 26*

I've learned that even at the age of forty-nine, you can still feel like a twelve-year-old child when your mother is talking to you.

—*Age 49*

I've learned that if you pretend like you're taking notes, the teacher won't call on you.

—Age 18

I've learned that the size of a house has nothing to do with how happy it is inside.

—Age 22

I've learned that once a relationship is over, if you experienced more smiles than tears, then it wasn't a waste of time.

—Age 26

I've learned that it's those small, daily happenings that make life so spectacular.

—Age 21

I've learned that when a friend has had a fight with a spouse, he or she can call them every name in the book, but you had better not or you're in big trouble.

—Age 65

I've learned that if you cut your meatloaf into pieces, your parents will think you ate some of it.

—Age 11

I've learned that you shouldn't always bail your children out of trouble even though you may want to.

—Age 47

I've learned that I cannot blame my parents for my problems anymore!

—Age 24

I've learned that boys only rub your back to find out if you are wearing a bra.

—Age 11

I've learned that my grown children remember and treasure the things we did rather than the things we bought. —*Age 65*

I've learned that I don't have a right to complain about something if I had the power to change it and didn't. —*Age 22*

I've learned that my older brother does not like me to fold his underwear. —*Age 18*

I've learned that whatever else you like to cook, people will remember your homemade soups and biscuits. —*Age 49*

I've learned that mothers don't have time to be sick.
                                              —*Age 32*

I've learned that money doesn't buy class.
                                              —*Age 44*

I've learned that when I awake aching in various joints and thinking "Oh, what's the use?" if I get out of bed, don some clothes, splash cold water on my face, put on a little lipstick—I can face the world for another day!
                                              —*Age 86*

I've learned that we should be glad God doesn't give us everything we ask for.

—Age 18

I've learned that if you wouldn't write it down and sign it, you probably shouldn't say it.

—Age 21

I've learned that you need to close the door to your house before you rescue a chipmunk from your cat.

—Age 52

I've learned that after all these years, I still have a crush on my husband. —*Age 28*

I've learned that when my parents say, "It doesn't matter what we think, you are the one dating him"—they hate the guy. —*Age 24*

I've learned that the thing that gives me the most joy is writing to my eighty-three-year-old sister. —*Age 86*

I've learned that I shouldn't weigh myself every day when I'm on a diet.   —*Age 21*

I've learned that grandmothers are mothers with a second chance.   —*Age 58*

I've learned that when I can't sleep in the middle of the night, I find great joy in watching my husband and children sleeping peacefully.   —*Age 37*

I've learned that life is like a roll of toilet paper. The closer it gets to the end, the faster it goes. —*Age 66*

I've learned that nothing is really work unless you would rather be doing something else.

—Age 85

I've learned that it doesn't matter how young you are when you get married, as long as it is to the right person.

—Age 22

I've learned that simple walks with my father around the block on summer nights when I was a child did wonders for me as an adult.

—Age 18

I've learned that a lonely place in your heart can be filled by volunteer work.

—Age 54

I've learned that the way a child enters a house after school tells you how his day was.

—Age 65

I've learned that when my spouse has failed to fulfill my needs, it's highly likely I've also neglected his.

—Age 32

I've learned that a nap in a hammock on a summer's day is the best sleep ever invented.

—*Age 21*

I've learned that sometimes all a person needs is a hand to hold and a heart to understand.

—*Age 19*

I've learned that all people have both good and bad traits. The secret of a happy marriage is to concentrate on your spouse's good traits.

—*Age 60*

I've learned that when my dog does *his* job,
I feel relieved!

—Age 56

I've learned that older people in my family
have a wealth of knowledge to share if I
just ask and listen.

—Age 26

I've learned that you should take a wet
washcloth in a Ziploc bag on field trips.

—Age 44

I've learned that it really doesn't hurt a child to go to bed without a bath.   *—Age 32*

I've learned that the more mistakes I make, the smarter I get.   *—Age 13*

I've learned that no matter how serious your life requires you to be, everyone needs a friend to act goofy with.   *—Age 21*

I've learned that if you are happy, it is because you put others before yourself.

—Age 86

I've learned that when coming home from college, if your little brother wrestles you to the ground, it's his way of telling you he loves you. *—Age 19*

I've learned that you can never be too good a listener when a friend is in need. *—Age 13*

I've learned that if you share your garden, you will be rewarded tenfold. —*Age 44*

I've learned that you should never say no to a gift from a child. —*Age 54*

I've learned that I can always pray for someone when I don't have the strength to help him in some other way. —*Age 76*

I've learned that when my baby thinks he is hungry, it doesn't matter what I think.

—*Age 37*

I've learned that you should never eat a Butterfinger in front of a hungry dog.

—*Age 11*

I've learned that our background and circumstances may have influenced who we are, but we are responsible for who we become.

—*Age 25*

I've learned that there's nothing better on a rainy day than soup, television, and a nap on the couch.

—Age 21

I've learned that a good way to get your house clean is to invite someone over for dinner.

—Age 50

I've learned that using a dollar's worth of gas to save twenty-five cents on a crosstown purchase is poor economics.

—Age 46

I've learned that the best time to go through your brothers' stuff is when they are not at home.

—*Age 12*

I've learned that you can kill a cockroach with hairspray.

—*Age 19*

I've learned that having three teenage sons at the same time in the same household is as close to temporary insanity as I ever want to be.

—*Age 39*

I've learned that the best way to succeed is to do small things well.

—*Age 68*

I've learned that my wife's cooking is always good, no matter how bad it is.

—*Age 31*

I've learned that nothing beats a hot summer night, a car full of friends, the windows down, music playing, and whistling at boys!

—*Age 18*

I've learned that the best time to ask your dad if you can do something is when he's sleeping.

—Age 11

I've learned that you should never wear your swimsuit on a two-hour ride in the car.

—Age 9

I've learned that children sleep better if they have had a hug and a kiss from both mom and dad.

—Age 60

I've learned that scratches on furniture made when your children were little are fond memories when they are grown and gone.

—Age 72

I've learned that the janitor is the most important person in the building. —*Age 54*

I've learned that you can say anything you need to say if it is done in kindness. —*Age 47*

I've learned that my father saved me from many a foolish act with these words: "Go ask your mother." —*Age 16*

I've learned that being kind is more important than being right.

—Age 34

I've learned that I need to let my friends comfort me and hold me up, to let them know I need support, that I'm not always as strong as I look or act.

—Age 49

I've learned that when I'm waiting to see the doctor, I always wish I had stuck to my diet.

—Age 47

I've learned that as soon as you get rid of something you haven't used in years, you need it the very next week. —*Age 38*

I've learned that words harshly spoken are as difficult to retrieve as feathers in a gale.

—*Age 60*

I've learned that sometimes when my friends divorce, I'm forced to choose sides even when I don't want to. —*Age 44*

I've learned that you should always accept a foreign exchange student into your home if given the chance.

—Age 37

I've learned that one sincere apology is worth more than all the roses money can buy.

—Age 40

I've learned that there is nothing like the feel of warm mud between your toes.

—Age 22

I've learned that I should not eat jalapeños
the night before traveling.   *—Age 37*

I've learned that just because two people
argue, it doesn't mean they don't love each
other. And just because they don't argue, it
doesn't mean they do.   *—Age 22*

I've learned that if you stick a piece of ice
down a boy's pants, he screams bloody
murder.   *—Age 10*

I've learned that all grandchildren are beautiful, brilliant, and take after their grandparents.

—Age 65

I've learned that what we have done for ourselves alone dies with us. What we have done for others and the world remains and is immortal.

—Age 89

I've learned that people will remember you as being a great conversationalist if you mostly listen.

—Age 49

I've learned that there is a great feeling of independence when you buy your first silverware.

—Age 23

I've learned that having a child fall asleep in your arms is one of the most peaceful feelings in the world.   —*Age 22*

I've learned that having a party when your parents are out of town is taking a great risk.   —*Age 15*

I've learned that although I didn't understand the principles of gravity in high school physics, I do now when I look at my body at age fifty.   —*Age 50*

I've learned that the best classroom in the world is at the feet of an elderly person.

—Age 47

I've learned that flipping through the channels is not annoying if I hold the remote.

—Age 42

I've learned that I shouldn't write anything in a letter that I wouldn't want printed on the front page of a newspaper.

—Age 67

I've learned that just one person saying to me, "You've made my day!" makes my day.

—Age 20

I've learned that when I mentally list all the little joys the day has brought me before I fall asleep, I rarely have a sleepless night.

—Age 44

I've learned that I feel better about myself when I make others feel better about themselves.

—Age 18

I've learned that there is a great thrill in making pickles and jellies with the same friend I used to make mud pies with. —*Age 60*

I've learned that I should never let my little brother take me for a ride in the golf cart.

—*Age 11*

I've learned that even men love to be romanced once in a while. —*Age 19*

I've learned that if you hang something in a closet for a while, it shrinks two sizes.

—Age 62

I've learned that little boys cannot move about the house without making car sounds.

—*Age 36*

I've learned that being quiet doesn't always mean you have nothing to say.   —*Age 17*

I've learned that when you are really stressed out, the cure is to put two miniature marshmallows up your nose and try to "snort" them out.

—*Age 11*

I've learned that it's all worth it when you are doing a sink full of dishes and your eighteen-year-old comes up behind you and gives you a big hug. And you ask, "What was that for?" And she replies, "No special reason."

—*Age 42*

I've learned that there's always room for dessert.

—*Age 12*

I've learned that when you're in love, it shows.

—*Age 28*

I've learned that there is nothing more soothing than the sound of a piano on a sunny Sunday morning.

—Age 32

I've learned that whenever my mom calls me on the phone to say "hi," it always makes me smile.

—Age 20

I've learned that a kindness done is never lost. It may take a while, but like a suitcase on a luggage carousel, it will return again.

—Age 77

Dear Reader,

If life has taught you a thing or two and you would like to pass it on, please write it down with your name, age, and address and mail it to me. I would welcome the opportunity of sharing it with other readers in a future book. Thank you!

H. Jackson Brown, Jr.
P.O. Box 150014
Nashville, TN 37215